FEB 2021

For Bill and Sharon,
my Drosselmeyer and Sugar Plum Fairy —J.R.A.

For my friend Liam Miller —R.D.

May you leap from these pages to
the world's great stages —American Ballet Theatre

Text copyright © 2020 by John Robert Allman
Jacket art and interior illustrations copyright © 2020 by Rachael Dean

All rights reserved. Published in the United States by Doubleday, an imprint of Random House
Children's Books, a division of Penguin Random House LLC, New York.

Doubleday and the colophon are registered trademarks of Penguin Random House LLC.

American Ballet Theatre, ABT, America's National Ballet Company, and the ABT Logo are registered
trademarks of Ballet Theatre Foundation, Inc., dba American Ballet Theatre. www.abt.org

Visit us on the Web! rhcbooks.com

Educators and librarians, for a variety of teaching tools, visit us at RHTeachersLibrarians.com

Library of Congress Cataloging-in-Publication Data
Names: Allman, John Robert, author. | Dean, Rachael, illustrator. | American Ballet Theatre.
Title: B is for ballet : a dance alphabet / by John Robert Allman ; illustrated by Rachael Dean.
Other titles: At head of title: American Ballet Theatre presents
Description: First edition. | New York : Doubleday Books for Young Readers, [2020] |
Audience: Ages 3–7. | Summary: "An alphabetic celebration of the world of ballet"
—Provided by publisher.
Identifiers: LCCN 2020009535 (print) | LCCN 2020009536 (ebook)
ISBN 978-0-593-18094-5 (hardcover) | ISBN 978-0-593-18095-2 (library binding) |
ISBN 978-0-593-18096-9 (ebook)
Subjects: LCSH: Ballet—Juvenile literature. | Alphabet books. |
English language—Alphabet—Juvenile literature.
Classification: LCC GV1787.5 .A45 2020 (print) | LCC GV1787.5 (ebook) | DDC 792.8 [E]—dc23
MANUFACTURED IN CHINA
10 9 8 7 6 5 4 3 2 1
First Edition

AMERICAN BALLET THEATRE
presents

B IS FOR BALLET

A Dance Alphabet

By John Robert Allman

Illustrations by Rachael Dean

Doubleday Books for Young Readers

Lucia Chase in *Les Sylphides*

A is for the arabesque,
a quintessential pose,
performed with outstretched arms and legs
and perfect, pointed toes.

B is for the ballet barre, where dancers learn to balance,
and also for Baryshnikov's extraordinary talents.

Mikhail Baryshnikov (in photos), Aran Bell, and Calvin Royal III

C is for the company, beginning with the corps,
then soloists and principals, who make *Coppélia* soar.

D is for the daring dances done by Ms. de Mille.
Rodeo's rowdy ranchers strut with swagger and with skill.

E's for épaulement, which makes a simple stance impressive.
Just turn your head and shoulders, and a pose is more expressive.

Isabella Boylston in *La Bayadère*

F is for those famous, flawless, feverish fouettés.
Swan Lake's Odile does thirty-two, which set the stage ablaze.

Gillian Murphy in *Swan Lake*

G is for glissade, a step that comes from French for "glide" and moves the sweet and sorrowful Giselle from side to side.

Natalia Makarova in *Giselle*

H is for the hairdo that helps ballerinas stun:
on stage or in rehearsal, it's a tight and tidy bun.

I is for an ice bath, soothing tired, tattered feet.
After promenades in pointe shoes, relaxation can't be beat.

Allesandra Ferri

J is for jeté, ballet's most beautiful of bounds.
Petit or grand, this joyful jump assuredly astounds.

Christine Shevchenko in *Le Corsaire*

K's for Kenneth and for Kevin,
dancers turned directors,
coaches, choreographers,
and pirouette perfectors.

Kevin McKenzie and Kenneth MacMillan

L is for the leotards
that ballerinas wear
to illuminate their lines
as partners lift them in the air.

Julie Kent and Kevin McKenzie

M's for modern masterworks,
whose movements break the mold,
and also Misty Copeland,
always brilliant and bold.

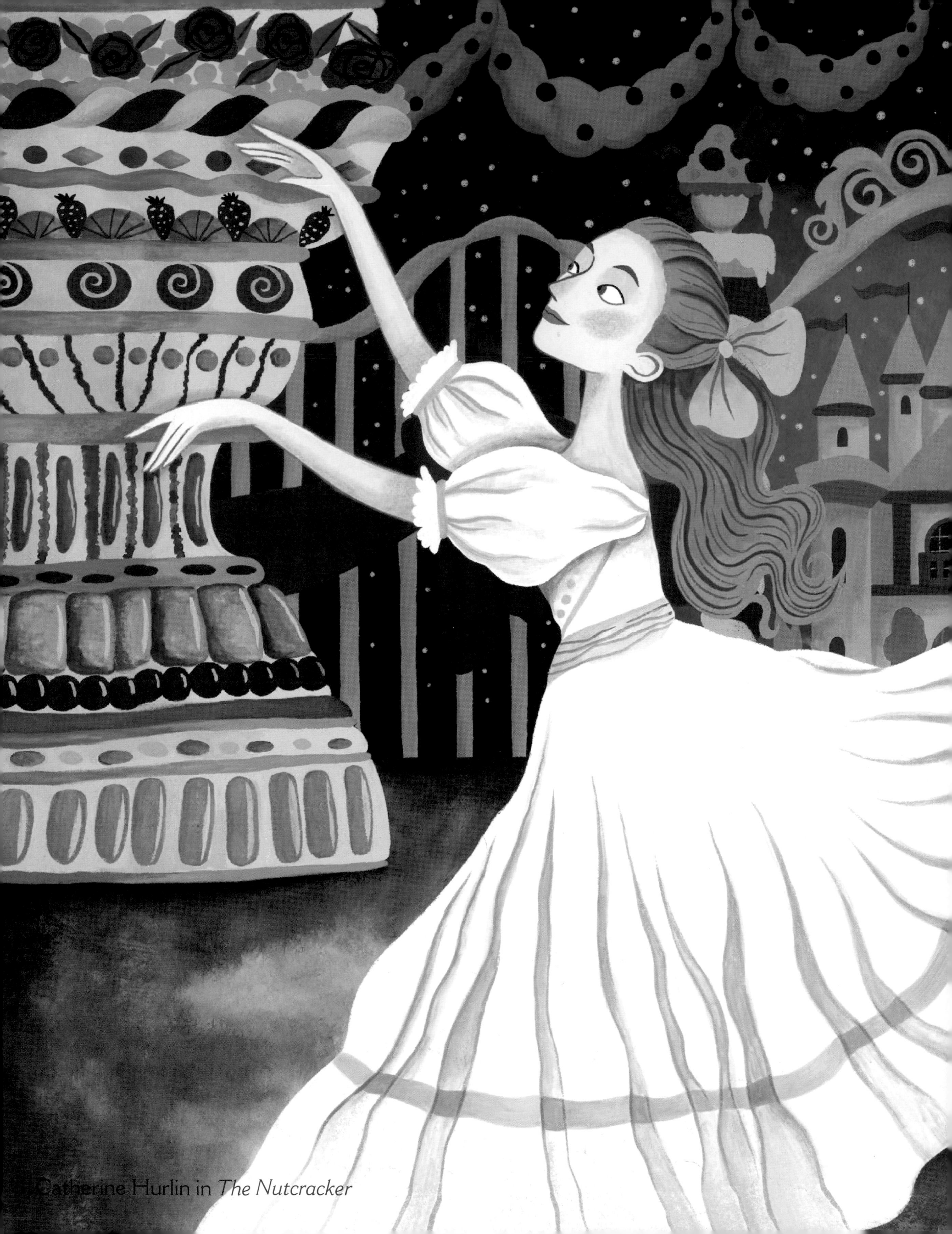

Catherine Hurlin in *The Nutcracker*

N is for *The Nutcracker*,
a holiday tradition.
Join Clara in the Land of Sweets
right after intermission.

O is for the orchestra,
which gives the ballet wings,
making music wonderfully
on woodwinds, brass, and strings.

The American Ballet Theatre Orchestra

1st   **2nd**

P is for the five positions dancers must perfect.
Before pliés or relevés, your feet must be correct.

3rd   4th   5th

Students at the ABT Jacqueline Kennedy Onassis School

Q's for *Don Quixote*
(which for short is called *Don Q*).
Watch Kitri and Basilio
duet to say "I do."

Paloma Herrera and Angel Corella in *Don Quixote*

R is for the révérence as crowds cheer at the Met
and the final curtain falls on *Romeo and Juliet*.

S is for the stretching dancers do when they're off-duty
so they're stellar when they're starring in Ratmansky's *Sleeping Beauty*.

Sarah Lane

T's for Mr. Tudor's work, theatrical and thrilling.
His poignant pas de deux are charming, challenging, and chilling.

Twyla Tharp directing Cassandra Trenary, Herman Cornejo, and Skylar Brandt in *In the Upper Room*

U's for *In the Upper Room*,
sensational and sharp,
a contemporary classic
brought to life by Twyla Tharp.

V is for the virtuosic
Theme and Variations,
a vital one of Balanchine's
balletic innovations.

Igor Youskevitch and Alicia Alonso in *Theme and Variations*

W's for warming up
to keep from getting sore
when waltzing in three-quarter time
to *Cinderella*'s score.

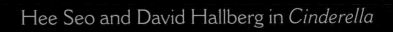

X is for extension,
which helps lift the leg up high
so that Cinderella's prince can point
his toes toward the sky.

Y is for the years and years
of diligent devotion
it takes to dance with elegance,
exactness, and emotion.

Z is for the zeal of fans who love the ballet so
and shout enthusiastically, "Bravi! Brava! Bravo!"

You now know ballet's basics and can dance from A to Z
in class, on stage, or cheering for the next ballet you see!

TERMINOLOGY

arabesque (ah-ruh-BESK) · A pose on a straight or bent supporting leg, with the other leg extended straight and behind.

artistic director · The creative leader of a ballet company.

barre · A railing that dancers hold for balance when warming up.

"Bravi! Brava! Bravo!" (BRA-vee, BRA-vah, BRA-vo) · Italian for "well done," shouted by audience members to express their admiration: "brava" for a woman or girl, "bravo" for a man or boy, and "bravi" for both.

bun · Hair pulled back into a tight coil.

choreographer · The creator of a dance's steps and other movements.

company · A ballet troupe's full roster of dancers: principals, soloists, and the corps de ballet.

corps de ballet (kor duh bal-AY) · The dancers in a ballet company who perform as a group.

duet · A dance performed by two people.

épaulement (ay-pole-MON) · Twisting the upper body and shoulders and tilting the head to extend the line of a ballet position.

extension · A dancer's ability to raise and hold a leg in the air.

fouetté (fweh-TAY) · A whipping movement of a raised leg, usually paired with a pirouette.

glissade (glih-SAHD) · A gliding step, beginning and ending in a fifth-position plié.

ice bath · A treatment used by dancers and other athletes to relieve muscles after intense exercise.

intermission · A break between acts of a performance.

jeté (zhuh-TAY) · A leap involving the transfer of weight from one foot to the other, including grand (or large) and petit (or small) jetés.

leotard · A close-fitting garment often worn by dancers.

lift · Holding another dancer in the air.

line · The shape created by the body in a position or movement.

modern ballet · A genre (also known as contemporary ballet) that blends elements of classical ballet and modern dance.

orchestra · A group of string, woodwind, brass, and percussion instrumentalists.

pas de deux (pah duh duh) · A dance performed by two people.

pirouette (peer-uh-WET) · A full turn performed on one foot, on demi- (or half-) pointe or full pointe.

plié (plee-AY) · Bending one or both knees, either halfway (demi) or fully (grand).

pointe (poynt) · Performing on the tips of the toes in pointe shoes.

positions · The five basic positions of the feet. (Various schools and methods use different arm positions.)

principals · A ballet company's highest-ranking dancers, who perform leading roles and solos.

promenade (prom-en-AHD) · Turning slowly in place on one foot while maintaining a pose, by making slight movements of the heel. In a *pas de deux*, holding your partner and walking around them to spin them in a pose.

relevé (reh-luh-VAY) · Rising on the toes of one or two feet.

révérence (ray-vay-RAHNS) · A bow or curtsy to thank a teacher or audience.

score · The musical composition that accompanies a ballet.

soloists · The dancers who rank above the corps de ballet but below the principals, performing featured roles and solos.

stretching · Flexing and extending muscles to improve elasticity and tone.

waltz · A sweeping dance to music composed in three-quarter time.

warming up · Exercises and stretches before dancing to prevent injury.

BALLETS

La Bayadère · With music by Ludwig Minkus, *La Bayadère* was originally choreographed by Marius Petipa and premiered in St. Petersburg, Russia, in 1877. Set in India, it tells the love story of a temple dancer, Nikiya, and a noble warrior, Solor.

Coppélia · Set to music by Léo Delibes and based on stories by E. T. A. Hoffmann, *Coppélia* was originally choreographed by Arthur Saint-Léon in Paris in 1870. It is a comic ballet about a handsome youth, Franz; the village beauty, Swanilda; and a life-size doll, Coppélia.

Le Corsaire · *Le Corsaire*, about a dashing pirate's love for a beautiful young woman, premiered in Paris in 1856, with a score by Adolphe Adam and choreography by Joseph Mazilier.

Don Quixote · Based loosely on Miguel de Cervantes's novel, *Don Quixote* debuted in Moscow in 1869, with music by Ludwig Minkus and choreography by Marius Petipa. It centers on the romance between Basilio and Kitri, and on the idealistic title character who aids them in their quest to marry.

Firebird · First performed by the Ballets Russes in 1910, with a score by Igor Stravinsky and choreography by Michel Fokine, *Firebird* tells the tale of a magical creature who helps two lovers overcome an evil sorcerer. It was reimagined by ABT in 2012, with choreography by artist-in-residence Alexei Ratmansky.

Giselle · *Giselle* premiered in Paris in 1841, with choreography by Jean Coralli and Jules Perrot and a score by Adolphe Adam. When Giselle falls in love with and is deceived by Albrecht, she dies of a broken heart. The Wilis, spirits of other betrayed young women, attempt to dance Albrecht to death, but Giselle saves him from beyond the grave.

In the Upper Room · *In the Upper Room* is an athletic, bold modern ballet choreographed by Twyla Tharp in 1986, to a score by Philip Glass.

Jardin aux Lilas · With choreography by Antony Tudor set to music by Ernest Chausson, *Jardin aux Lilas* premiered in London in 1936. It centers on Caroline, who is engaged to be married, at her pre-wedding party.

The Nutcracker · Based on an E. T. A. Hoffmann story, *The Nutcracker* premiered in St. Petersburg in 1892, with choreography by Marius Petipa and Lev Ivanov and a score by Pyotr Ilyich Tchaikovsky. Set on Christmas Eve, it follows a young girl and a wooden nutcracker who turns into a prince. ABT's newest production was choreographed by Alexei Ratmansky.

Rodeo · Choreographed by Agnes de Mille to a score by Aaron Copland, *Rodeo* debuted in New York City in 1942. It stars an enthusiastic cowgirl on a ranch with rowdy male cowhands.

Romeo and Juliet · Based on Shakespeare's tragedy, *Romeo and Juliet* premiered in 1938 in Brno, Czechoslovakia, with a score by Sergei Prokofiev and choreography by Ivo Váňa-Psota. It has been reinterpreted by many choreographers, including Antony Tudor, John Cranko, and Kenneth MacMillan, whose acclaimed production has been performed at ABT.

The Sleeping Beauty · *The Sleeping Beauty* premiered in St. Petersburg in 1890, with a score by Pyotr Ilyich Tchaikovsky and choreography by Marius Petipa. It has been restaged by Kenneth MacMillan and Alexei Ratmansky, among others.

Swan Lake · With music by Pyotr Ilyich Tchaikovsky and choreography by Julius Reisinger, *Swan Lake* debuted in Moscow in 1877. It stars one ballerina in the dual roles of Princess Odette, the White Swan, and Odile, the Black Swan, who attempts to sway Prince Siegfried's love for Odette.

Les Sylphides · *Les Sylphides* is a romantic work with music by Frédéric Chopin and original choreography by Michel Fokine. It was first performed by the Ballets Russes in Paris in 1909.

Theme and Variations · With choreography by George Balanchine set to music by Pyotr Ilyich Tchaikovsky, *Theme and Variations* is a celebration of the Imperial Russian Ballet. It was first performed in 1947 by New York's Ballet Theatre, which later became ABT.

CHOREOGRAPHERS

George Balanchine (1904–1983) · Considered the father of American ballet, George Balanchine was born in St. Petersburg, Russia. After dancing with and choreographing for the Ballets Russes and other companies, he moved to the United States, where he cofounded both the School of American Ballet and New York City Ballet.

Agnes de Mille (1905–1993) · Agnes de Mille was a groundbreaking choreographer in ballet and on Broadway. Her work includes ballets *Rodeo*, *Three Virgins and a Devil*, and *Fall River Legend* and Broadway shows *Oklahoma!*, *Carousel*, and *Brigadoon*, for which she won a Tony Award.

Kenneth MacMillan (1929–1992) · Kenneth MacMillan served as artistic director and then principal choreographer at London's Royal Ballet for over two decades. He also staged numerous ballets for ABT and was its artistic associate director from 1984 to 1989.

Kevin McKenzie (1954–) · Kevin McKenzie joined American Ballet Theatre as a soloist in 1979. He was promoted to principal in 1980, danced with ABT until 1991, and has served as the company's artistic director since 1992.

Alexei Ratmansky (1968–) · Alexei Ratmansky was born in St. Petersburg, Russia, and trained at the Bolshoi Ballet School in Moscow. He was the artistic director of the Bolshoi from 2004 to 2008. In 2009, he became ABT's artist-in-residence and has since choreographed seventeen ballets for the company.

Twyla Tharp (1941–) · Twyla Tharp joined the Paul Taylor Dance Company as a dancer in 1963 before founding her own company, Twyla Tharp Dance, in 1965. She also created and staged numerous ballets for ABT and was its artistic associate director.

Antony Tudor (1908–1987) · A giant of twentieth-century choreography, Antony Tudor choreographed for ABT's inaugural season in 1939 and remained associated with the company for the rest of his life. His landmark works include *Pillar of Fire* and *The Leaves Are Fading*.

DANCERS

Stella Abrera (1978–) · Stella Abrera began her career as a member of ABT's corps de ballet in 1996. She was appointed a soloist in 2001 and a principal in 2015.

Alicia Alonso (1920–2019) · Born in Havana, Cuba, Alicia Alonso overcame near-blindness to deliver legendary performances, particularly as the title role in *Giselle*, for Ballet Theatre (later ABT) in the 1940s. In 1948, she returned to Havana and founded the Alicia Alonso Ballet Company, which became Ballet Nacional de Cuba.

Mikhail Baryshnikov (1948–) · Mikhail Baryshnikov is widely regarded as one of the best male ballet dancers in history. He began his career with St. Petersburg's Kirov (now Mariinsky) Ballet. After defecting to the West in 1974, he rose to international fame as a principal dancer with ABT. He served as the ABT's artistic director from 1980 to 1989. An advocate for modern dance, Baryshnikov cofounded White Oak Dance Project with Mark Morris in 1990 and launched the Baryshnikov Arts Center in 2005.

Aran Bell (1998–) · Aran Bell joined the ABT Studio Company in 2014 and the main company as an apprentice in 2016. He became a member of the corps de ballet in 2017 and was appointed a soloist in 2019.

Isabella Boylston (1986–) · Isabella Boylston joined ABT's Studio Company in 2005, became an apprentice with the company in 2006, and was promoted to the corps de ballet in 2007, to soloist in 2011, and to principal in 2014.

Skylar Brandt (1993–) · Skylar Brandt joined ABT II (now ABT Studio Company) in 2009. She became a member of the main company as an apprentice in 2010 and joined the corps de ballet in 2011. In 2015, she was promoted to soloist.

Lucia Chase (1907–1986) · Lucia Chase cofounded Ballet Theatre—which changed its name to American Ballet Theatre in 1957—with Richard Pleasant in 1940. She retired from dancing in 1960 but stayed with ABT until 1980, when she retired as company director.

Misty Copeland (1982–) · Misty Copeland joined ABT Studio Company in 2000, becoming a member of the company's corps de ballet in 2001 and a soloist in 2007. In 2015, she was promoted to principal dancer, becoming the first African American woman to achieve this position in ABT's history.

Angel Corella (1975–) • Angel Corella danced with ABT from 1995 until his retirement in 2017. Since 2014, Corella has served as the artistic director of the Pennsylvania Ballet.

Herman Cornejo (1981–) • Herman Cornejo danced with Ballet Argentino before joining ABT's corps de ballet in 1999. He was promoted to soloist in 2000 and to principal in 2003.

David Hallberg (1982–) • David Hallberg joined ABT Studio Company in 2000 and became a member of the corps de ballet in 2001. He was promoted to soloist in 2004 and principal in 2006.

Catherine Hurlin (1996–) • Catherine Hurlin joined ABT Studio Company in 2012. She then joined the main company as an apprentice in 2013 and the corps de ballet in 2014, and was appointed a soloist in 2018.

Paloma Herrera (1975–) • Paloma Herrera joined ABT's corps de ballet in 1991. She was promoted to soloist in 1993 and principal in 1995. In 2017, she became artistic director of Ballet Estable del Teatro Colón in Buenos Aires.

Julie Kent (1969–) • Julie Kent joined ABT as an apprentice in 1985. She was promoted to the corps de ballet in 1986, to soloist in 1990, and to principal in 1993. Julie was named artistic director of The Washington Ballet in 2016.

Natalia Makarova (1940–) • Among the most celebrated ballerinas of her time, Natalia Makarova began her career with the Kirov (now Mariinsky) Ballet. In 1970, she defected from the Soviet Union, joining ABT as well as performing with London's Royal Ballet. In 1983, she made her Broadway debut in *On Your Toes*, for which she won a Tony Award.

Gillian Murphy (1979–) • Gillian Murphy joined ABT's corps de ballet in 1996 and was promoted to soloist in 1999 and principal in 2002.

Calvin Royal III (1989–) • Calvin Royal III joined ABT II (now ABT Studio Company) in 2007. He joined the main company as an apprentice in 2010 and the corps de ballet in 2011, and was appointed a soloist in 2017.

Hee Seo (1986–) • Hee Seo joined ABT Studio Company in 2004. She joined the main company as an apprentice in 2005 and was promoted to the corps de ballet in 2006, to soloist in 2010, and to principal in 2012.

Christine Shevchenko (1988–) • Christine Shevchenko joined ABT's Studio Company in 2006 before joining the main company as an apprentice in 2007 and the corps de ballet in 2008. She was appointed a soloist in 2014 and a principal in 2017.

Cory Stearns (1985–) • Cory Stearns began his career with the ABT Studio Company in 2004. He became a member of the main company as an apprentice in 2005, and was promoted to the corps de ballet in 2006, to soloist in 2009, and to principal in 2011.

Devon Teuscher (1989–) • Devon Teuscher joined ABT's Studio Company in 2006 and the main company as an apprentice in 2007. She was promoted to the corps de ballet in 2008, to soloist in 2014, and to principal in 2017.

Cassandra Trenary (1993–) • Cassandra Trenary joined ABT II (now ABT Studio Company) in 2011. She joined the main company as an apprentice, became a member of the corps de ballet in 2011, and was promoted to soloist in 2015.

James Whiteside (1984–) • James Whiteside began his career with Boston Ballet II in 2002 before joining the Boston Ballet's corps de ballet in 2003. He was promoted to second soloist in 2006, first soloist in 2008, and principal in 2009. Whiteside then joined ABT as a soloist in 2012 and was appointed a principal in 2013.

Igor Youskevitch (1912–1994) • Igor Youskevitch was one of the greatest male dancers of twentieth-century American ballet. He trained and danced with companies including the Ballets Russes de Monte Carlo before enlisting in the U.S. Navy and becoming an American citizen in 1944. In 1946, he joined Ballet Theatre (later ABT), where he performed for nine years, frequently alongside partner Alicia Alonso.